What's Wrong With My Plants?

Carl Brack, Sr.'s Guide for Vegetable Gardening

Vabella Publishing
P.O. Box 1052
Carrollton, Georgia 30112
www.vabella.com

The information in this book is compiled from the author's lifetime of learning about gardening via printed material, educational courses, conversations with fellow gardeners of all levels of expertise, and personal experience and, to the best knowledge of the author and publisher, is written in the author's own words. Any part of this book that may appear to be plagiarized is purely coincidental. The author and publisher have made every effort to ensure that the information in this book is originally written and correct. The author and publisher do not assume and hereby disclaim any liability to any party for any loss, damage, or disruption caused by errors or omissions, whether such errors or omissions result from negligence, accident, or any other cause.

Manufactured in the United States of America

Library of Congress Control Number: 2016901975

13-digit ISBN 978-1-942766-07-0

Front cover photos by Janet Reid.

Special thanks to Kelly Green and Susan Mashburn.

10 9 8 7 6 5 4 3 2 1

To Steve Davis and Johnny Tanner

Preface

Gardening is valuable in many different ways. Many of us think of gardening as for the production of food. Of course it is, but it is also for the soul. Gardening makes us closer to our great Creator. Only He can create life. When we put what appears to be dead seed in the soil, we see the miracle of life come forth, we feel that we have helped God just a little bit in that new life.

It is also a means of therapy for us. It simply makes us feel better than any other job we may perform. Maybe it is because we were made from the soil, and life was breathed into us, so we are at home and peace there.

How about exercise? We know how important it is to each of us to keep our body in good shape to ensure a longer life. However, exercise for the sake of exercise is hard. It is not as rewarding because we are not producing something. It is simply making us tired. In the garden we are getting exercise and enjoying every minute of it. The earliest and biggest tomato is just around the corner, the family and the neighbors will be fed—enough to make one feel good.

How about the disabled and poor? Produce from our gardens can, and does, keep the food pantries of the community open longer to provide more assistance to those in need.

Keep your garden as a place of enjoyment and relaxation. Do not make it a chore. The biggest reason there are one year gardeners is because they made their garden bigger than the time they had to spare.

I have had an enjoyable and rewarding experience writing this book. I hope this book helps you to have a rewarding and enjoyable experience in your gardening endeavors.

Carl Brack, Sr.

Introduction

This book is intended to be a guide for new and experienced gardeners on the management of different vegetables that we grow in the garden.

It discusses the different vegetables, their environmental needs, fertility needs, insect and disease problems, and physiological problems. Much of the information discussed will be scientific information based on thirty years of training of the author through his profession as a County Agricultural Agent with the University of Georgia Cooperative Extension Service. After retiring from the University of Georgia he worked nine years part-time at Goldkist Garden Center, eleven years part time with Southern States Garden Center, and is presently working part-time at Southern Home and Ranch—all located in Carrollton, Georgia. The author also works as a private consultant.

Some of the information may even be classified as "Old Wives Tales." They are called this because they have no scientific background. However, through a basic understanding of plant needs we can see how some of these remedies do actually work. Others may appear to be useless, but still it is helpful to know them so as not to be taken in when someone tells you what they call a new remedy.

A portion of this book deals with some of the more than 40,000 questions answered by the author. During his years as a County Agent, he had the opportunity to answer over 40,000 questions, recorded over 5,000 radio programs, wrote over 1,200 news articles and gave hundreds of lectures. These experiences provided an opportunity to hear the real questions that people want answers to.

In the question and answer sections, the author wants to answer those questions not easily found in textbooks and planting guides. The questions and answers are shown with the applicable crop.

Explanation of gardening terms used in this book

Composting – Collecting organic materials in a pile or a structure to breakdown into organic matter which may be plowed into the soil to improve structure and provide nutrients.

In the drill – Drill is the same as row. It may be used as, "The seeds need to be spaced 8 inches in the drill (row)."

Mulching – Applying organic material to the top of the soil around plants to improve growing conditions by preventing weeds, improving moisture holding and preventing soil-borne diseases, etc. May be plowed back in to improve the soil.

Recycling – Adding organic matter back to the soil to improve fertility and tilth.

Rotation – Moving families of plants to different areas of the garden as much as feasible. Examples are following peas with corn or following squash with beans.

Seedbed – An area of soil that has been specially prepared to receive seed or plants. The area has been plowed deep, fertilized, limed and organic matter has been applied.

Side dress – Adding fertilizer to the side of the plants in the row. Usually recommended six weeks after planting.

Tilth – "Plow-ability" of the soil. Good tilth means the soil is crumbly and plows easily.

Top dress – Adding fertilizer to the top layer of soil.

Table of Contents

RECYCLING

Gardeners are some of the original recyclers. Most gardeners knew before it became popular that it was helpful to add leaves and other organic matter back to the soil.

There are many different methods of recycling. One of the easiest is to put some leaves on the soil in the fall and turn them under. They will have the winter and possibly some of the spring to decompose. They should not be applied to a depth of more than 3 to 4 inches over the garden. The addition of lime and fertilizer at that time will aid in the decomposition process.

There are many different containers that may be used to make a compost pile, but a container does not have to be used. The leaves and other materials may simply be piled up and nature will take its course. Containers that may be used include a circle of wire, 4 pallets tied together or a 6x6 square made of boards. Containers may be purchased that can be turned by hand to speed up the process. Garbage bags may be used. Leaves may be put in the bags in the fall. Water, seal, and you have compost next spring.

Whichever method is used, the addition of garden soil and fertilizer will aid in decomposition. Any garden soil has the organisms that are capable of breaking down organic material. The fertilizer provides food for the organisms to multiply. Commercial materials may be purchased containing these organisms.

Once the material is decomposed it may be used as a mulch or it may be worked into the soil.

Most any organic material may be used in the compost pile. Some household items such as bones should not be used as they encourage animals to dig into the pile. Avoid weeds with seed heads as this will make weed control more difficult. It is wise not to put in much slow decomposing materials such as pine straw. Save some of this and use it for mulching. It can then be used for compost the second year.

MULCHING

Mulching is the addition of some organic material to the top of the soil to prevent weeds, hold water, moderate soil temperature and prevent fruit diseases by keeping the fruit from touching the soil. It will also prevent soil splashing up on the fruit and infecting them with soil-borne diseases.

There are many materials that may be used for mulching purposes. Some of these include leaves, sawdust, lawn clippings, shavings, pine-bark, hardwood bark or pine straw.

It is best to water the garden prior to applying the mulch. It should be applied to a depth of about 3-4 inches when settled. After the season is over mulch may be composted the next year. It also can be removed and used again the next year. It may be turned under; if it has a high percentage of pine straw, it will cause planting and cultivating problems the next spring. Two manmade materials have come on the scene in the last few years. These included black plastic and fabric materials. The plastic is much cheaper. When it is used the row middles are left uncovered. These areas may be mulched with straw, hay or some material that will allow air and water to penetrate.

The fabrics are more expensive, but may be removed and used over and over. They have many advantages. They will allow nutrients, air, and water to pass through. It makes side dressing and watering much easier.

ASPARAGUS

Asparagus is one of those plants that is permanent as long as you want it to be. Because it is a perennial that comes back from the roots each year, you will want to plant it in a spot in the garden where it will not get in the way of tilling and other gardening activities. A corner in the garden usually makes a good place.

Soil preparation is very important in establishing an asparagus bed. A good seedbed should be prepared a few weeks prior to planting. This is best done by digging furrows fifteen inches deep and about that wide. Plant as many rows as needed about 4 to 5 feet apart. The asparagus will spread and fill in between rows. Asparagus loves organic material. Rotted sawdust, leaves or other organic material should be placed in the bottom of the furrow to a depth of 2 to 4 inches. Add the same amount of topsoil. Mix lime and fertilizer with the other ingredients. Apply about one pound of 1-2-3 (5-10-15) fertilizer and two pounds of agricultural lime per 10 feet of row. Add another 2 to 3 inches of topsoil. Purchase well rooted crowns that are one year old. They should be planted 15 inches apart. Finish covering the trench with topsoil. It will settle after a while. More topsoil should be added as the shoots emerge.

Asparagus needs time to get a good root system established. Because of this spears should not be harvested the first year. The spears should be allowed to develop into ferns. These ferns will manufacture food for root growth, and storage for next year's growth. As soon as they turn brown in the fall they may be cut back, as food has already been stored in the root system.

The second year spears may be harvested for 1 week. The third year spears may be harvested for 2 weeks. Spear harvest may be increased 1 week per year until the tenth year. Continue harvesting at that rate.

Management of asparagus is very important. Fertilizer should be applied each year at the same rate shown above. It is also important to keep the pH up to 6 to 6.5. Lime will be needed periodically to adjust the pH.

ASPARAGUS Q & A

Q. My asparagus ferns have turned brown this fall. My neighbors say I should wait until next spring to cut them back. When is the proper time?

A. It is important that you wait until they turn brown before you cut them. This shows they have taken the nutrients out of the upper portion of the plant, and stored them in the roots for next year's growth. They may be cut back any time after they turn brown.

Q. I planted my asparagus last year. I did not harvest any spears. Is it proper management to harvest a portion of them this year?

A. It is important that you harvest spears for 1 week this year. You left the spears last year so as to let more energy go to establish a more extensive root system. This year, by harvesting for 1 week, you have the benefit of some asparagus, but quit harvesting after that period so the plant will have time to recover and continue to develop a root system. Next year, which will be the third year, you may harvest for two weeks. Continue increasing 1 week each year until about the age of ten years. Continue at this rate.

BEANS

The term bean refers to a multitude of different plant shapes and edible fruit. The plants may be low growing bushes, vines that will grow many feet long or anywhere in between. They are referred to as bush beans, pole beans or half runners. The pole beans are grown on poles or some other type of support. Half runners are usually not supported.

Beans are also divided into categories as to the part of the bean that is eaten. The beans which the pods are eaten are called green beans, snap beans, or string beans. The type which the edible parts are eaten is called butter beans or lima beans. There are many different varieties in each of these categories.

In the green bean, snap bean, string bean category there are different varieties. Some of these are bush type and some are pole type. In some varieties there may be a bush and a pole type. The different varieties may have different color pods such as green or yellow. They may be string or string-less.

A bean that fits more in this category but the bean is eaten is called the horticultural or October bean.

The lima bean differs from green beans in both size and color. There are pole and bush type in the Lima varieties. Only the bean is eaten in the Lima category. There are many different sizes. The beans may vary from one half inch to as much as an inch in length. All sizes are tender if harvested at the proper stage of development.

Limas also differ in color. Some varieties are a pale green, some are speckled and some are colored beans. There are different colors in bush and pole beans.

Warm weather is required for all of these beans. They should not be planted until after the last frost of the season. Many gardeners plant the green beans 10 to 14 days earlier than Limas. It seems they will tolerate more cool weather and cool soil than Limas.

Beans are in the legume family. They can manufacture their own nitrogen. Because of this, a fertilizer low in nitrogen should be used. They are moderate users of fertilizer. Even though they are legumes many gardeners feel they will produce more if they are side dressed when production starts declining.

Bush beans are planted about 3 inches apart, and pole beans are planted about 12 inches apart. They should be planted in 36 inch rows about one inch deep.

The major insects that attack beans are the Mexican Bean Beetle, bean leaf beetle and the cowpea curcullio.

Sanitation is the first step in preventing these insects. Destroy all old plants as soon as harvest is over. Keep fence rows clean to prevent overwintering of insects. Insecticides can be used to control all of these insects. The cowpea curcullio must be prevented by spraying during the bloom stage. The moth punctures the pod and lays the egg immediately after bloom. Once the egg is inside most treatment is futile.

The snap bean type should be harvested before the seed bulges and while the pod is still tender, as that is the part that is eaten. The lima bean should be harvested after the seed is swollen but before it starts turning yellow.

BEANS

The horticultural bean should not be harvested until the purple stripes on the sides are very pronounced. Since the seed of this bean is the edible part it needs to be mature. If they are harvested too early they are very difficult to shell.

Two of the many diseases that affect beans are rust and anthracnose. Rust only affects the leaves, but anthracnose will penetrate the beans making them rot. Some gardeners have difficulty distinguishing between the two. Rust will turn your fingers or pants legs brown. Anthracnose does not have this characteristic. Any fungicide that will control anthracnose will control rust.

BEANS Q & A

Q. My beans came up, but they died like they were rotting off at the soil line. What can I do to cure or prevent this?

A. You can't do much for these beans. If a large percentage of the beans show the symptoms you have stated, you will need to replant. Cold damp soil increases the incidence of this fungal caused disease. It is called damping-off. It is best to wait until the soil is warm before planting. It also helps to treat the seed before planting with fungicides such as Captan or Terrachlor. Sometimes the plants will survive and be hollow on the inside like it has been hollowed out by an insect. When this happens the stem will be black at the base or have a black steak.

Q. My beans look like they have rusty spots on the leaves. What causes this, and what can I do to control it?

A. Rust is one disease that can be cured with fungicides after it has become established. Most diseases have to be prevented or treatment started very early. The first thing to do is to rub the spots between your fingers. If the brown spot comes off on your fingers then it is rust. If it does not come off on your fingers then the problem is Anthracnose. This disease is more serious, as it attacks the seed pods, penetrates and causes the beans to rot. If it is rust, treat with sulfur. If you determine the problem is Anthracnose, you will need to treat with a recommended fungicide.

BEETS

Beets can be produced in the garden. They are a cool season crop that should be planted in the fall or early spring. They do not like hot weather, so they should be harvested prior to summer heat.

Beets are usually planted as seed in the garden. A good seedbed is recommended. The seed should be planted in 30 to 36 inch rows and 2 inches apart. Some gardeners prefer planting 1 inch in the drill. They thin the plants to 2 inches and use those removed for greens. One inch is usually the depth planted.

Control the weeds by mulching. Pulling, hoeing, plowing or chemicals may also be used.

BEETS

Beets like a pH of 6 to 6.5. They are medium users of fertilizer. The fertilizer should be applied in split applications. They like small amounts of boron, sulfur and zinc.

There are not many insects and diseases that affect beets. The main insect is the flea beetle, and they can be controlled with insecticides.

The major diseases are blights, leafspots and downy mildew. They should be treated with fungicides when the first signs appear.

The leaves of beets may be harvested when they are 4 to 6 inches in length. The roots should be harvested when they are about 2 inches in diameter and before the heat of the summer.

BROCCOLI

Broccoli is a cool season plant that has increased tremendously in gardens during the last 20 years.

It is one of the few plants in which the flower is the part of the plant that is consumed. The blooms are harvested in the immature stage while they are still tender. Once the blooms open they are no longer edible.

The plants are planted in the garden after being seeded about six weeks earlier. Broccoli can be panted in the early spring or fall. A hard freeze will kill the plants. They can withstand a light freeze or frost. Some enthusiastic gardeners plant in early spring. They are prepared to cover the plants with milk jugs or some other cover if the weather demands. Containers like milk jugs trap some of the soil heat and keep the frost off the plants. An extreme cold spell will still kill the plants.

When planted it is a good management practice to water the plants with a solution high in phosphate. Young plants need phosphate, and cool weather seems to limit the intake of this particular nutrient.

The plant is a heavy user of all major nutrients, so it should be fertilized as a heavy user including topdressing. The topdressing should be applied when the plants are 10 to 12 inches tall. A complete analysis fertilizer should be used for this application.

Many gardeners apply another application of nitrogen when the bloom starts and another to help side shoots develop after the main head is harvested.

The young leaves harvested with the head are usually good to eat, but the older leaves should be discarded.

There are a number of insects that attack broccoli, but the one most irritating to gardeners is a small green worm that does not show up until they are in hot water. That is when they are in the pot. They suddenly show up on top of the water. This can be eliminated by soaking the heads in warm salty water thirty minutes prior to cooking.

Another problem in young plants is the cut worm. It can be eliminated mechanically by wrapping aluminum foil loosely around the plants 2 inches above and 2 inches below ground level. Other insects should be identified and treated with the proper insecticide.

Biological control with agents, such as Bacillus thuriengiensis, is one of the safest control methods since the bacteria used in this control is only harmful to caterpillar type insects.

BROCCOLI Q & A

Q. My broccoli put up yellow flowers when it was only a few inches high. What can I do to save my broccoli?

A. There is nothing you can do. This is known as "bolting." It may happen to broccoli, cabbage, collards, and cauliflower. This is the fear of all commercial producers. It can destroy all their crops and cause financial ruin. It is thought to be caused by warm conditions during the growing of the plants. It will not do any good to break off the flowers.

Q. Should I harvest the center and side heads at the same time?

A. Not necessarily. If left, the side shoots will enlarge after the main head is harvested. Both the main head and side shoots should be harvested before the buds begin to open. It will lose its flavor and become tougher once the opening process begins.

BRUSSEL SPROUTS

Brussel sprouts are another one of those vegetables whose production and consumption has increased, especially in the south as people migrate from one part of the country to another.

Growing conditions for Brussel sprouts are very similar to those for broccoli production. The edible part of the Brussel sprout is a small cabbage head that is produced in the axil of the leaves.

The seed is first grown indoors about six weeks prior to planting in the garden. They are usually planted in early spring or fall. The plant can withstand some cold and even light frost. When a heavy freeze is expected the plants should be covered.

The plant is a heavy user of fertilizer. A complete analysis fertilizer should be used at planting. A second application of complete fertilizer should be applied 3 to 4 weeks later. Topdressing with nitrogen is beneficial every 3 to 4 weeks until harvest.

Cutworms and cabbage loopers are two of the most troublesome insects that attack brussel sprouts. A barrier such a aluminum foil placed around the stem at planting time will prevent cutworms.

Cabbage loopers can be controlled with a number of insecticides when they are small. The larger the worm, the harder they are to control. Many gardeners say they get best results from the biological control Bacillus thuriengiensis.

BRUSSEL SPROUTS

The harvesting of the head is very important. They should be harvested when they are still bright green. Once they begin to lose color they become tough. The heads are harvested from the bottom up. The leaves should be removed from as far up as the heads are removed. This will stimulate growth of heads farther up the plant.

A major problem in brussel sprouts, broccoli and cabbage is a physiological problem called "bolting." This is when the plant blooms while it is immature. Sometimes the plant is only 3 to 4 inches tall. The reason for this early blooming is not completely understood. Some researchers think bolting may be caused by becoming too warm during the early growth period.

Once this phenomenon occurs nothing can be done to reverse this development. The plant should be destroyed.

CABBAGE

Cabbage is a cool season crop that can be planted in late winter or late summer. They thrive in cool weather and can tolerate some frost.

Cabbage is usually planted in the garden as plants. They are usually planted as seed in the greenhouse 6 to 7 weeks before they are planted in the garden.

Cabbage likes a pH of 6 to 6.5, and they are heavy users of fertilizer. The lime, if needed, should be applied 3 to 6 months prior to planting. One half the fertilizer should be applied at planting time with the remainder being applied 6 weeks later. Cabbage is usually planted in 30 to 36 inch rows 12 inches in the drill. To prevent cutworms, the stem should be wrapped with aluminum foil at planting time. Cabbage, like most plants, responds well to a starter fertilizer. A starter fertilizer is usually high in phosphorous. Phosphorous does not move much in the soil, so this additional phosphorous provides the limited root system of small plants a better opportunity to come in contact with it. The starter solution is usually applied in the water at planting time. A gardener may make his own starter solution by dissolving one tablespoon of garden fertilizer in a gallon of water. Pour the water off leaving the granules which may be applied to the soil. The solution should be used to water the plants.

Weeds may be controlled by herbicides, plowed, hoed or pulled. There are now herbicides that will kill the grass even after it is up, and it will not damage the cabbage.

Cabbage is subject to a number of insects and diseases. The major insects are cabbage maggot, cabbage looper, diamond moth, imported cabbage worms and harlequin bugs.

The maggot is a soil insect and must be controlled by applying the proper insecticide before planting. It also helps to wait until the soil warms up and is sufficiently dry. Some gardeners report good results from putting a mesh over the plants to prevent the moth from laying eggs at the base of the plant.

The other insects may be treated with insecticides since they attack the leaves.

Disease affecting cabbage includes wire stem, black rot, foliar diseases, downy mildew and alternaria leafspot.

Blackspot is the most difficult to control. Once it is established in a crop, not much can be done. The home gardener should be sure to buy certified plants. Wirestem usually occurs in plants placed in warm soil in the summer. It is best to wait until the soil is cool or apply a fungicide when the plants are put in the garden.

The foliage diseases can be controlled by starting a spray program when they are first observed.

Cabbage may be harvested when the head is formed. Too much water causes the heads to split.

There are a number of varieties of cabbage. Some of these include the flatheads, roundhead, hybrid, savoy and many others.

CABBAGE Q & A

Q. My cabbage made large heads this year but they split open. What did I do wrong?

A. I can't say whether it was you or Mother Nature, but someone applied too much water. This is what caused the heads to split.

CANTALOUPE

The cantaloupe is in the cucurbit family. This is the family where the fruit precedes the bloom on the female bloom. The male and female parts of the plant are completely separate. Like the other members of this family, bees are a must for pollination to take place.

Cantaloupe prefers a pH of 6 to 6.5. They are medium users of fertilizer. The fertilizer should be applied in split applications. Some gardeners prefer to make three applications.

They should be planted on beds about 5 to 6 feet apart. Since they are vines that run, the rows should be about 4 to 6 feet apart. The seed should be planted 1½ inches deep.

Weeds, especially grass, can be a problem in cantaloupe production. The grass can be controlled by plowing, hoeing, pulling or with chemicals.

There are very few pre-emergence chemicals recommended on cantaloupes. Those that are can only be purchased in large quantities for commercial use. Recently, post emergence herbicides have been developed that will control grasses after they have emerged. These chemicals have proved quite adaptable to small gardens.

Insects can be a problem on cantaloupes from the time they are planted until they are harvested. The spotted and striped cucumber beetle will attack the seedlings before they emerge from the soil. They may also carry a serious bacterial disease called bacterial wilt. They can be controlled with a good insecticide program.

Leaf miners can also be a problem. The main symptoms are the white trails that appear on the leaves. The leaf miners do not usually cause severe damage, but they provide a entry point for disease organisms. They can also be controlled with insecticides.

The pickle worm can be a serious problem. They eat all parts of the plant, from the bud to the mature fruit. They bore into the fruit and push out a sawdust like material. They must be controlled before they enter the fruit. Once in the fruit control is impossible. Insecticides must be used to prevent the insect from entering the fruit.

Another insect that is a problem is the squash vine borer. They attack young and old plants. They bore into the vine at the soil line, and the plant rots off at that point. Applications of insecticides applied seven days apart are required to control this insect. Many gardeners pull soil to the vine periodically. The vine puts on roots higher up on the plant. If it is already being attacked below this point these roots will help it survive. The larvae may be removed from the vine by hand if found in time.

Cantaloupes are also affected by a number of diseases. All of these diseases can be prevented with a good spray program. A good rotation program will help prevent the diseases. Cucurbits should not be planted in the same area more than once every three years. Variety selection is also very important as some are more disease resistant than others.

Cantaloupes are ready to harvest when they turn from pale green to pale yellow. The netting also becomes more pronounced.

CANTALOUPE Q & A

Q. I planted cantaloupes this year. They started out fine, and then the runners started wilting and dying one at a time. They continued until the whole plant died. I ended up losing almost all of the plants. What did I do wrong or what caused this?

A. This sounds like a fungal caused disease named gummy stem blight. Some of the newer varieties are more disease resistant that the old ones. You should use Western grown seed. At the first sign of the disease you should start a program using a good fungicide recommended for this disease.

Q. How can I tell when my cantaloupe is ripe?

A. The stem will easily separate from the fruit. The fruit will lose its greenish color. The netting will become more pronounced.

Q. My cantaloupes are covered with blooms, but there are very few melons. What is the problem and what can I do about this?

A. First, it is impossible for over 50% of the blooms to make a fruit. This is because at least that many and probably more are male blooms. The male blooms come on the plant first. This is nature's way of making the pollen ready when the female blooms are open. Check your vines to see if the female blooms are on the vine. They can be recognized by the small fruit coming out ahead of the bloom. The male blooms will sit directly on the stem. If there are plenty of female blooms on the plant and open, the problem must be caused by a lack of pollination. This is done by bees which are short in some areas. The only answer to this problem is to bring in bees. If the problem happened to be a lack of female blooms patience is the answer. Nature will correct that problem.

CARROTS

Carrots are one of the most attractive plants in the garden. The fernlike tops and the golden roots are quite easy to grow. They are very rich in vitamin A. Because of the elongated root system the soil should be loamy down to a depth of 8 inches or more. There are some varieties that have a shorter root and are larger in diameter. If the soil is not properly prepared, especially for the longer varieties, the carrot will be malformed.

Carrots are cool season plants, so they should be planted in the fall or early spring. They may be planted in rows or in a bed. The seed are very tiny. A good way to spread them is to tear off one corner of the package and shake them out. The rows should be 24 to 30 inches apart, and 2 to 3 inches in the drill. The small seed should be planted about ¼ inches deep.

Since carrots are a cool season plant, the weed problems are not very bad. As with most other crops, the weeds can be controlled by pulling, hoeing, plowing or mulching.

Carrots are medium users of fertilizer and does best in a pH of 6 to 6.5. Split applications of fertilizer should be used. Carrots also need boron, sulfur and zinc.

Carrots, depending on the variety, may be harvested as soon as they are large enough to eat. They should be harvested before heat of summer, and fall plantings should be harvested before frost.

CARROTS Q & A

Q. I planted carrots that I thought would be 6 to 8 inches long. They turned out to be short and stubby. What caused this?

A. It may be that you accidently got some variety that does not grow long. Some gardeners prefer these, especially if they have hard clay subsoil. Also if you have hard subsoil, and didn't prepare it deep enough this could have been the problem. To make your soil loamier you should add an organic material such as peat moss and work it in.

CAULIFLOWER

Cauliflower is a cool season plant that may be planted in the spring or fall. The part of the plant eaten is called the curd.

Cauliflower is usually planted in the field as plants that are six to seven weeks old. The seed are usually started in a greenhouse so they will be ready for planting after the last hard freeze in the spring. For fall planting, it should be planted early enough to mature before the first hard freeze.

Cauliflower likes a pH of 6 to 6.5. It is a heavy user of fertilizer. A pop-up fertilizer is recommended at planting time. The fertilizer should be applied in split applications. Cauliflower also likes small amounts of boron, sulfur and zinc.

Weeds may be controlled by plowing, pulling, hoeing, or with chemicals. In small gardens the most effective method is to use mulch which may be turned under the following year.

There are diseases that may attack cauliflower from planting until harvest. These include blackleg, black rot, club gall and fusarium wilt.

The best control for most of these diseases is rotation and sanitation.

Club root can be prevented by using a fungicide in the water at planting time.

There are a number of insects that attack cauliflower. Some of these include aphids, cabbage loopers, cutworms, flea beetles and root maggots.

Root maggots should be treated in the soil at planting time using an insecticide for soil insects. Cutworms can also be controlled with aluminum foil wrapped around the stem at planting. The other insects are leaf feeders. They should be controlled as the need arises.

The curd should be blanched when it is about the size of a quarter. This is done by pulling the outer leaves over the head and securing with a rubber band. There are some varieties that are self-blanching. They have been somewhat successful. They have leaves that grow up over the curd.

Cauliflower should be harvested before the curd begins to divide. Late harvesting will cause the curd to taste grainy or ricey. Leaving some of the leaves on when harvested helps to retain quality.

CAULIFLOWER Q & A

Q. I grew cauliflower in my garden this year. It grew well, but it was yellowish colored and had an unusual taste. It didn't look and taste like that I buy in the grocery store. What does this sound like?

A. The problem is you did not blanch the head or curd as it is called. The sun causes these problems you mentioned. To blanch you pull some of the leaves over the curd when it is about the size of a quarter or earlier. You can use the flat rubber bands to hold the leaves in that position protecting them from the sun. There are now some self-blanching varieties where the leaves grow upright, and protect the curd from the sun. They do a fair job according to some gardeners.

COLLARDS

Collards are a very versatile plant. They may be planted in the fall or spring since they are cool season plants. It has higher fats, proteins and carbohydrates than most other greens.

Collards prefer a pH of 6 to 6.5. They are medium users of fertilizer. Split applications of fertilizer are recommended. Topdress with nitrogen if needed. They respond well to a pop-up fertilizer if the plants are used in the field instead of seed.

The plants are produced from seed that are sown in the greenhouse transplanted in the field when they are about 6 to 7 weeks old. In the fall, some gardeners sow them like turnips and thin when large enough. They can take frost and some freezing temperature. Some say frost enhances the flavor.

Collards make fairly large plants if they are allowed to mature. Because of this the plants are planted in 30 to 36 inch rows and spaced 10 to 12 inches in the drill.

Those gardeners who sow directly in the field usually thin to the distances above. If larger plants are not desired, the leaves may be cropped. More leaves will be produced like turnips and other greens.

There are many different varieties. They may be as high as 36 inches. One variety makes a head which somewhat resembles a cabbage.

Once planted, the first problem is weed control. This problem is not as significant as it is for warm season crops. The weeds that do germinate can be controlled by the conventional methods or with chemicals.

There are a number of insects and diseases that affect collards. The main diseases that affect collards are Alternaria leafspot and Downy Mildew. At the first sign of disease a spray program should be started with the recommended fungicide.

Insects that attack collards are aphids, cabbage loopers, cabbage webworm, flea beetles, root maggots and others. Most of these insects can be controlled with a good spray program. To control root maggots a soil insecticide should be applied before planting.

Collards may be harvested as soon as the leaves are large enough to eat, or they may be harvested when they are mature.

COLLARDS Q & A

Q. I am growing collards in my garden. Do I have to harvest the whole plant at one time?

A. No. Individual leaves may be harvested. The bud will continue to produce new growth.

Q. I have been successful growing collards except for a small green worm that is very difficult to control. What is this insect, and how can I control it?

A. This insect is a cabbage looper. They are indeed hard to control, especially when they get close to maturity. Many gardeners say it is very difficult to control this insect with the old standby Sevin and the other insecticides used in the garden. Many gardeners and commercial growers are now using a biological control method. This is Bacillus thuringiensis. It is a disease organism that affects only a certain type of caterpillars. It is sold under names such as Dipel, Thuricide and Asana XL, etc.

CORN

Corn was planted in America long before Europeans came here. It was one of the staples of the American Indian. It was easy to grow and easy to keep over the winter.

Today's corn looks quite different from that grown by the Indians. Because of selection and hybridization, the quantity of corn has been greatly improved in the last fifty years.

Today's gardener may select sweet or field corn. There are many different varieties of each. Sweet corn has some more sugar, and field corn has more starch.

Corn is usually planted in furrows. Later, soil is thrown to the row. This helps to support the corn which does not have tap roots. It only has lateral roots which are support roots. It can be planted early. Hard freezes will kill the plant, but it can tolerate a frost to the point of burning off the leaves. It has a "hidden bud" which is protected because it is down in the plant. Corn needs to be planted about 2 inches deep. This is deeper than most plants. It is a medium user of fertilizer. It is recommended that after applying a complete analysis fertilizer at planting, additional nitrogen be applied when the plant is 12 to 18 inches tall. Additional nitrogen is needed because it takes corn so long to mature. It takes corn from 75 to 120 days to mature. Corn should be planted in 36 inch rows with 8 to 10 inches between the hills. It also helps to apply about one tablespoon of zinc sulphate and borax per 100 foot of row. Because of the small amount these two elements are best applied in water.

One of the major insects that affect corn is the corn earworm. It is one of those insects that must be prevented. Once it is inside the ear it is almost impossible to control.

The biological control Bacillus thuringensis and other insecticides may be used to control this insect. Some gardeners say to apply about two drops of mineral oil on the silks as soon as they form. It is supposed to affect the eggs that are laid by a moth.

The harvesting of corn is very important for quality. It should be harvested when still in the milk stage. This is best determined by pulling the shuck back and puncturing the grain with the fingernail. The juice should be milky and squirt in all directions. The grains should be fully formed. It should be added that another indicator of maturity is the turning brown or black of the silks.

When corn is harvested, the sugar starts turning to starch immediately. Therefore, it is best to harvest in early morning while it is still cool. The ears should be cooled to 35 degrees and processed as soon as possible.

CORN Q & A

Q. Why do my corn plants have a purple color?

A. This is the symptom of phosphorous deficiency. It especially shows up when corn is planted early. Phosphorous is not as available in cold weather, probably because of slow root growth. Phosphorous is not very movable in the soil, so the roots have to go to it. It helps to add a pop-up fertilizer at planting time. This fertilizer should be high in phosphorous. Corn will eventually overcome the problem if there is sufficient phosphorous in the soil.

Q. I planted corn the same this year the same as usual, but it has many suckers. Will these suckers affect production, and should I remove them?

A. In the past, suckers have been removed from corn plants. In recent years, research has shown the suckers do not affect the corn. There is no reason to remove the suckers unless you want to do so to have a perfect garden.

Q. The corn crop in our garden looked perfect until the ears came on. Before long they were covered with a growth that looks like mushrooms or toad stools. It looks gross. Will it hurt my family to eat the corn if the growths are removed?

A. The growth you asked about is actually corn smut. It is related to toad stools and mushrooms. It is caused by a fungus, and what you see is a fruiting body. If left, it will dry up and affect next year's ears if all conditions are right. Some gardeners prepare the fruiting bodies as they would mushrooms and eat them. They are harmless to people. The corn can be eaten when the smut is removed. Some varieties of corn are much more susceptible to smut than other varieties. It is also much more prevalent in wet seasons.

Q. Why do the corn ears in our garden have only blisters and not any grains of corn?

A. Pollination is probably the problem. Under normal condition, corn does not have a pollination problem. But if the temperature goes above 95 degrees during pollination the pollen can be killed. In gardens, the problem is sometimes not enough stalks side by side for pollination purposes. This usually happens when only one or two rows are planted. There should be 5 to 6 rows planted together. Every grain must be pollinated separately in order for that grain to mature.

Q. Corn earworms are a problem in my garden. How can I control them?

A. Some gardeners tell me they can control them by putting two drops of mineral oil on the skills as soon as they are seen. The biological method of control is to use Bacillus thuringiensis. There are also a number of insecticides that can be used.

CUCUMBERS

Cucumbers are in the cucurbit family, same as squash, cantaloupes, pumpkins, gourds and watermelons. This family of vegetables is recognized by uniqueness of the small fruit forming on the plant before the bloom itself. The male and female blooms are completely separate. Because of this bees are very important for pollination.

Cucumbers like a pH of 6 to 6.5. They are medium users of fertilizer. Like the other cucurbits, cucumbers like small amounts of boron, sulfur and zinc.

They can be planted from seed, but in the last few years, more are being planted as plants. They may be planted in the field after the last frost or in late summer for a fall crop. Because of their vining characteristic, they are planted in rows 3 to 5 feet apart and 3 to 4 feet in the drill. Closer rows may be used if the cucumbers are trellised.

This saves much space and reduces disease problems. The seed should be planted about 1 to 1½ inches deep.

Weeds may be controlled by mulching, hoeing, plowing, pulling or with chemicals. The best method is mulching which also helps prevent diseases, conserves moisture, moderates soil temperature, and later provides organic material when worked into the soil.

There are many insects and diseases that affect cucumbers. They must be controlled if a crop is to be produced. Insects attacking cucumbers include spotted and striped cucumber beetles which may attack the seedling before it emerges and continue to eat holes in the leaves and flowers. A control program should be started early. Sanitation after harvest for the next year is important in their control. Chemicals may also be used.

Leaf miners seldom do a lot of damage, except the trails and spots they eat on the leaves may provide an entry point for disease organisms. The infected leaves may be removed by hand. An insecticide program is also needed. The pickleworms will attack all of the upper portions including the fruit. The most damage is done when they bore into the fruit. To avoid damage to the fruit they have to be prevented with a spray program.

The squash bug can weaken and even kill young plants. On older plants, they severely damage runners. Control includes picking off bugs and eggs, sanitation and applications of insecticides.

The squash vine borer attacks the plant at ground level and bores into the plant. It will usually rot off at that point.

The larvae may be dug out of the plant with a knife. Insecticides may be used applied at the base of the plant. Other methods of control include planting as early as possible and pulling soil to the plant. The latter will encourage new roots to put out even after the plant is damaged.

Diseases that attack cucumbers include Anthracnose, gummy stem blight, Downy and powdery mildew. All of these diseases can be controlled by applying one of the recommended fungicides.

Cucumbers also may be affected by environmental problems such as hot dry weather. Curled or malformed fruit may be caused by improper pollination. Each seed of a fruit must be pollinated, or that part of the fruit will not develop properly.

There are many different types of cucumbers. Some are especially suited for pickling. There are others that are suited more for eating because they are low in acid.

There are also two types of plants based on growth habit. The old type is a vining type. That is, it runs on the ground and takes up much space in the garden unless it is staked or put on a trellis. A few years ago, an upright plant was developed. Its growth habit is much like a yellow squash. There are many more varieties to choose from in the vining family. Harvesting of cucumbers is determined by the variety and how it is going to be used.

The burpless and slicing varieties grow longer than the pickling varieties and keep their eating quality. The burpless have a low acid content, which makes them more desirable to most people for eating raw. The size to harvest can be determined by looking on the seed label or checking them in the produce section of the grocery store. They should be harvested before the seed are mature.

CUCUMBERS Q & A

Q. My cucumbers bloom profusely. They lose many of these blooms. What can I do to make them hold all of the blooms?

A. This subject is discussed more thoroughly in the discussion on cantaloupes. They are both in the cucurbit family, so they have some of the same problems. Briefly, you are losing many of the blooms because they are male blooms. You could be losing some due to the absence of bees which pollinates them.

Q. My cucumbers are bitter. What causes this, and how can it be corrected?

A. It is thought to be caused by hot dry weather. Under gardening conditions, mulch to moderate soil temperature and add water when needed. The bitterness is shallow. Peeling will remove much of the bitterness.

Q. My cucumbers are beautiful, but the fruit is curved and knotty looking. What is wrong?

A. The same condition that causes bitterness is thought to case some these problems. Also, if the fruit is not properly pollinated, it will be malformed. Any seed not pollinated will cause that section of the fruit not to develop.

EGGPLANT

Eggplants are in the same family as tomatoes. It is not one of the favorite vegetables in the garden. This is probably because it is not a favorite on the table. It is a very attractive plant to grow. There does not seem to be an abundance of recipes that makes the eggplant a gourmet food. One unusual recipe uses the eggplant to replace oysters in stew. Some eggplant enthusiasts are convinced you cannot tell the difference if you don't see it in the stew.

Eggplant production techniques are the same as its sister plant, the tomato. It is usually planted about 6 to 7 weeks before the last frost. It is planted in the greenhouse so the plants will be ready to plant in the field after the last frost.

At planting time, it is suggested that aluminum foil be loosely wrapped around the plant to protect it from cutworms and the soil born oxygen loving disease, Southern blight. This is the same disease that attacks tomatoes and pepper.

Eggplants prefer a pH of 6.0 to 6.5. They are medium feeders in fertilizer requirements. They do make over a long period of time, so they will benefit from side dressing. They can be side dressed with nitrogen or a complete analysis fertilizer high in nitrogen.

Due to the size of the fruit, many gardeners find it beneficial to support the plant with stakes or by some other means. A heavy fruit set can pull the plant over especially during wet weather.

During the last few years, new varieties of different shapes and colors have been developed. The original was a deep purple with a length about one and a half times its width. There are new varieties that are white and black. Some of the new varieties are one and two times as long as they are wide.

There are a number of insects that attack eggplants including the cutworm which has already been discussed. Some of the others include blister beetle, hornworm, leaf miners, flea beetles, spider mites and white flies. These insects can be controlled with insecticides applied at the right time.

Eggplants can be harvested from the time they are as large as a lemon until they are fully mature. They should be harvested before they start to change colors.

EGGPLANT Q & A

Q. As soon as I plant my eggplants, small holes appear in the leaves. What causes this?

A. The problem is the flea beetle. It is a tiny insect that is a beetle, but it jumps like a flea. They are the number one problem on eggplants, but they can be controlled with periodic applications of an insecticide such as Sevin.

Q. My eggplant died suddenly. There are white balls at the base of the plant. What is the problem, and how can I control it?

A. The cause of this is a fungal disease called Southern Blight. This can be prevented by wrapping the base of the plant with aluminum foil at planting time. The pustules are fruiting bodies of the disease. The fungi is oxygen loving. It must attack the plant at ground level. There is not enough oxygen below the soil surface for it to survive. The foil mechanically keeps the fungus away from the base of the plant. Do not throw soil over the foil during cultivation. Soil above the protection barrier will make plant susceptible to the disease. The foil will also protect the plant from cutworms. The other night shade plants, such as tomatoes, potatoes and pepper, are susceptible to this disease.

ENGLISH-GARDEN-EDIBLE POD PEA

These peas are all in the same family. In most instances, English and garden peas, as well as green peas, are the same peas. The edible pod pea is different but may be allowed to mature and be eaten like the other peas. Usually, it is harvested while young and the pod is snapped and eaten. These are the hardiest plants in the garden. They are planted in winter or spring as soon as the soil is workable. They can tolerate freezing temperatures; however they can be frozen out. They cannot tolerate hot temperatures.

English or garden peas may have smooth or wrinkled seed. Both of these have advantages and disadvantages. The smooth pea is more cold tolerant but has a higher percentage of starch which is undesirable. The wrinkled pea must be planted later, but, according to most gardeners, it is a sweeter pea which means it has a higher sugar content.

The edible pod pea must be sweeter than either because the varieties of this pea are associated with sugar, such as the variety Sugar Snap. It is thought to have gotten the name snow pea because they could be planted while the snow is still on the ground.

Another way of classifying this family of peas is by the stalk types. There are determinate type plants which means they are short. There are indeterminate types that grow taller and need support.

These peas are also in the legume family but do not need to be inoculated with a nitrogen fixing bacteria. They need a pH of 6 to 6.5. They do need more fertilizer than Southern field peas. They are in the medium category as to the fertilizer needs.

They should be planted about 1 inch deep and spaced about 1 inch in the drill. Close planting makes support for the indeterminate varieties easier. Support may be a fence or a few strings between posts in the row. They are not heavy like tomatoes and some of the other plants in the garden that need support.

The varieties to be shelled should be harvested when the seed inside fills out the shell. When the shell begins to change color, this is an indication that it is over mature and will be starchy. The edible pod peas should be harvested while the peas inside are still small. They can be sliced or snapped like beans. It is very important not to overcook when preparing.

GOURDS

Gourds are in the cucurbit family. It is difficult to distinguish between some squash and gourds. The luffa gourd is called running okra. It is also eaten. There are many different types of gourds, ranging from small ornamental gourds which are about 2½ inches in diameter to the gourd which may be 4 feet in diameter.

Gourds have many uses. The luffa is eaten, and it is also dried so the fibrous material can be used as a pot scrubber. Gourds are also used as bird houses, dippers, plant uses and for various other uses.

As mentioned earlier, they are in the Cucurbit family. This is the family that has separate male and female blooms. They will usually have many more male than female blooms. The male blooms will not produce gourds causing many growers to think something is wrong because so many of their blooms are not producing a fruit. Only female blooms produce fruit. They can be recognized by the small fruit coming on the vine before the bloom. Gourds are planted after the soil has warmed up. This usually happens in May or June. Because of their vining habit, gourds should be planted in 4 to 6 foot rows and 3 to 4 feet in the drill. The seed should be planted about 1 to 1½ inches deep.

Gourds may be provided a trellis or some other support system to keep them from taking up so much space in the garden. They may be planted in the corn after it is 4 to 5 weeks old. The corn will mature before the gourd competes for water and nutrients. They may be planted near a fence so they can run on it. One gardener planted in trash piles where trees had been bulldozed. This provided support. Certain types of gourd such as the dipper gourd need to hang down so the handle will be strait.

Some gardeners don't fertilize their gourds if they are planted in with other crops. They do respond to lime and fertilizer. Gourds like a pH of 6 to 6.5, and they are medium users of fertilizer. When fertilized, it should be done in split applications. If all the fertilizer is applied at planting time, they should be side dressed with nitrogen when about 6 weeks old.

Gourds are affected by the same insects and diseases that attack other cucurbits. Diseases include Downy mildew, powdery mildew and scab. A good spray program with recommended fungicides will prevent these diseases.

The most important insect attacking gourds is the fruit borers. They must be prevented by applying the proper insecticide to the fruit prior to infestation.

Gourds should stay on the vines as long as possible. They can be harvested as soon as the vine dies. This will usually happen before frost. The fruit should not be washed. It should be brushed off to remove all foreign material. They should be stored under a shelter with good circulation and off the ground. Some growers bore a small hole in the base of the bird house gourds to let the moisture seep out. This will aid in the drying process. The gourd is dry when the seeds rattle inside. The gourds may then be varnished or shellacked.

IRISH POTATOES

Irish potatoes are a staple in the diet of most Americans. It makes up a large percentage of the diet in many countries of the world. A potato blight in Ireland caused thousands of people to starve to death. Almost 25% of the people of that country migrated to other countries as a result of the blight.

Irish potatoes are planted in late winter or early spring. In some areas, they are also planted in late summer to make a crop before freezing temperatures come. They will tolerate a frost while they are young. If the tops are killed, they will put on new buds.

They will tolerate a lower pH than most garden plants. Their best pH range is 5.5 to 6.0. Potatoes do well at this range, however the fungus that causes scab does not thrive when the pH is on the upper side of that figure. Therefore, the disease damage is much less when the pH is kept within these bounds.

Potatoes are usually planted in a trench 6 to 8 inches deep. Some gardeners are reluctant to plant their potatoes that deep. There is a good reason for planting the seed pieces at that depth. Potatoes only make tubers above where the seed piece is planted. So there must be sufficient space between the seed piece and the soil surface for the tuber to make. The potato should not be on the soil surface exposed to the sun as we will discuss later.

There are many different variations as to how gardeners plant their potatoes. Some plant the seed piece in the furrow mentioned above. They then cover it with 2 inches of soil. As the plant grows then add old sawdust, peat moss, wheat straw, or other light organic material. As the tuber develops the small potatoes can be easily grappled. These young potatoes make very good eating. It also makes the harvesting process much easier.

Because potatoes are such heavy producers, they are classed as heavy users of fertilizer and should be fertilized as such.

Due to scab and other diseases, manure and other forms of organic material should not be worked into the soil. Fungi thrive in decaying organic material. This will make fungal caused diseases more acute.

Potatoes are produced from seed pieces that are cut from the tubers. The seed pieces should weigh one and one half to two ounces and have from one to three eyes on them. The eye is the bud where the potato will sprout.

Where the seed pieces are freshly cut makes an ideal media for disease organisms to grow and reproduce. It is good to cut the potatoes 18 to 24 hours before planting. This gives them the opportunity to cork over before they come in contact with the soil. It also helps to treat them with a fungicide before planting.

About the time they start blooming soil should be thrown to the base of the plant. This provides more depth for tuber production and keeps them out of the sunlight. This is very important because sunlight causes the formation of solanine acid. This is what causes the green potatoes you sometime see in the grocery store. There seems to be some difference of opinion as to how poisonous solanine acid is. It is known to cause throat constriction and choking. It is very soluble and is dissolved when the potatoes are cooked. The water should always be poured off. It usually does not penetrate very deeply, so it can be peeled away.

The blooming period is a critical time for water. Potatoes make such a tremendous poundage that large volumes of water is needed. Most all vegetables are made of mostly water. If possible they should be watered at this time.

The best time to harvest potatoes is when the vines begin to die. They should be plowed up and picked as soon as possible. They should not lay in the sunlight more than 30 minutes, as the solanine acid will start to form. They should be handled very carefully to avoid skinning and bruising. Any damaged potatoes should be used immediately and not put in with those to be stored.

Do not wash the potatoes at harvest unless they are to be prepared and frozen. Spring grown potatoes do not usually keep very long. If refrigeration were available, they would keep much longer. This is not usually possible for the gardener.

Brush the heavy soil from the potatoes, and spread them as thin as possible in a cool dry place. If crates are used make sure they have large cracks for air circulation. They should not be placed directly on plastic or concrete. Straw or some type of absorbent material should be placed under them. This helps to get the moisture away from the potato. Moisture increases rot problems.

There are a number of insects, diseases and physiological problems that affects potatoes.

An insect that most people are familiar with is the potato beetle. They can be controlled with a number of insecticides such as Sevin or Malathion.

Scab, mentioned earlier, is a disease problem along with fusarium wilt and nematodes. Crop rotation is the best system of preventing these diseases. Remember, potatoes are in the nightshade family same as tomatoes, pepper and the poisonous Jimson weed. It is important to remember that potatoes should not follow these crops as well as not following potatoes.

A physiological problem is the center of the potato cracking. This is usually associated with a heavy fluctuation of soil moisture and the heavy use of fertilizer.

IRISH POTATOES Q & A

Q. I am told I need to plant my Irish Potatoes 6 to 8 inches deep. Why is such deep planting necessary?

A. It is important because a potato only produces the tuber above where the seed piece is planted. If planted to shallow the tuber will not have enough space to develop, or they will be exposed.

Q. Why do people tell me to cut my potato pieces the day before planting?

A. A freshly cut potato is an ideal medium for all types of organisms to grow on. By cutting the potatoes the seed piece has time to cork over. This cork helps prevent the infection. It also helps to apply a fungicide to the seed piece at planting time.

Q. Last year my potatoes produced what appeared to be small tomatoes on the vine. My neighbor said it was because my tomatoes crossed with the potatoes. Is this true?

A. No, potatoes occasionally produce seed when all conditions are right. Many people have never seen this happen. The seed are capable of producing new plants. But, they sap strength from the tubers, so it is best to remove them from the plant when you see them.

Q. What causes my potatoes to turn green?
A. This happens when they are exposed to light. When they are being harvested they should remain on the ground only a short period of time. The green is solanine acid. It is poison. It causes a choking sensation. Potatoes with the green should be discarded or peeled deep. The acid is very water soluble, so boiling removes the acid. The water should be discarded.

LETTUCE

Lettuce is one of the easiest vegetables in the garden to grow. It is, however, very sensitive to hot weather. This is especially true of the heading types.

Lettuce is a cool season crop that will withstand some frost but not hard freezes. The heading types should be started indoors whether planted in the fall or spring. This gives it a good start so it can be planted outside in the moderated days of spring or fall. The heading type needs these extra days of moderate weather in order to mature. The tight lettuce like Iceberg and Crisphead are examples of those needing these extra days. Bolting or seed head formation will result if these types are grown in temperatures too high.

In addition to the tighthead lettuce there is another group called the loose-heading type. Two of these types include Butterhead and Bibb. Butterhead gets its name from its color. The leaves turn about the color of butter.

There is another group of lettuce, the Romaine or COS varieties. The leaves on these lettuces are curly, and they form loose upright heads.

The leaf type lettuces are the easiest of all to grow. They are harvested as soon as they are large enough to be eaten. Varieties of the leaf lettuces have green or reddish leaves depending on the variety.

Since lettuce cannot be stored for more than about two weeks, it is advisable to make small plantings at one to two week intervals. This will make fresh lettuce available over a longer period of time.

Lettuce is grown in rows. The heading type should be planted about 10 inches apart. The leaf type should be planted about 1 inch apart thinning as it is being used. The rows should be 24 to 30 inches apart. The seed should be planted about ½ inches deep.

Lettuce is a heavy user of fertilizer. A pH of 6.0 to 7.0 is the desirable range for lettuce. Split applications are recommended.

Diseases include downy mildew and bottom rot and drop. Both of these can be controlled with the proper use of fungicides.

Insects attacking lettuce include cucumber beetles, squash vine borer, pickleworms, squash bugs and others. These insects can be controlled with insecticides.

There are cultural problems that affect lettuce. These include bolting, bitter taste and tip burn. Bolting and bitter taste are caused by hot weather or water deficiency. It is thought that tip burn may be caused by low moisture or low calcium in the soil.

Weeds in lettuce are not usually much of a problem because of the time of year it is grown. The best method of control would be mulching. It helps keep the soil cool and prevents soil from being splashed on the leaves. This reduces the diseases such as leaf spot.

Lettuce is harvested depending on the type of lettuce it is.

The leaf lettuce is harvested as soon as the leaves are large enough to be useful. The outer leaves are desirable because they are high in calcium. Crisphead should be harvested when it looks like that in the grocery store. It will never have a head like cabbage. Bibb should be harvested when the leaves turn inward and begin to form a loose head. Cos or Romaine should be harvested when the leaves are 6 inches tall. Usually by that time, the heads will be somewhat tight but not as tight as crisphead.

LETTUCE Q & A
Q. What causes my lettuce to flower before it heads?

A. This is a physiological problem that is thought to be caused by warm temperatures. Once this happens the only solution is to replant.

MUSTARD

Mustard is a cool season plant that is similar to and planted about the same time as turnips. It may be planted in the fall or spring. Mustard can withstand light frost but cannot tolerate high temperatures. Some gardeners like to mix mustard, turnips, collards, kale and radish. They are all cooked together for variety.

Mustard may be planted in rows or on a bed. The smallness of the seed is referred to in the Bible. To plant the seed evenly they can be mixed with sand, lime or corn meal. This makes planting easier. It should be planted about 1 inch apart and cover to a depth of ¾ inches. If planted in rows they should be spaced 2 to 2½ feet apart.

Mustard likes a pH of 6 to 6.5. Mustard is a medium user of fertilizer. Split applications are best. If all the fertilizer is put down at planting time, the plants should be topdressed with nitrogen about 3 to 4 weeks after planting.

Weeds may be controlled by pulling, hoeing, plowing or with chemicals. Weeds are less of a problem with cool season plants. Mustard may be harvested as soon as the leaves are large enough, usually about 6 inches long. This will normally take 35 to 50 days.

Mustards, like other greens, have insects and disease problems. Insects include aphids, flea beetles and cabbage loopers. The loopers are the most difficult to control. Many producers are now using the biological control, Bacillus thuringiensis.

Diseases are about the same on mustard, turnips and collards. The primary diseases are cercospora, anthracnose and powdery mildew. To control spray with recommended fungicides at the first sign of disease.

OKRA

Okra is one of the most difficult plants in the garden to get up to a stand unless the gardener waits until the soil temperature is warm enough. This does not happen usually until May, because many gardeners cannot wait to get the seed in the ground.

There are many recommendations for improving germination. One of these is to put the seed in the freezer for at least 24 hours prior to planting. Others say a better method is to soak in warm water overnight, while others advocate soaking in Clorox overnight.

Most horticulturists agree that it is important to firm the soil over the seeds more than for most other seeds.

OKRA

Once okra germinates it is subject to root diseases, especially if the soil is cool. The plants rot off at the soil line and falls over. A good fungicide on the seed at planting will help prevent this problem.

Okra needs heavy fertilization because it produces profusely over a long period of time. It is said to be the only plant that will tell you when it needs more fertilizer, usually in the form of nitrogen. It will form a small cluster of blooms in the uppermost part of the plant. This indicates it needs to be side dressed with nitrogen or a high nitrogen fertilizer.

Once past the seedling stage, it does not have many insect or disease problems if a variety is planted that has a resistance to Fusarium wilt. It is affected by nematodes, a small microscopic worm that damages the root system, and causes the plant to lose its immunity to Fusarium. The worm injects a tube into the root and injects a fluid that breaks down the cell wall. The nematode then sucks the liquid back into its stomach where it is digested. The entrance made by the tube provides an entrance for the Fusarium fungus to enter. The plant starts turning yellow and finally dies. Okra should always be planted in an area free of nematodes or the soil should be treated prior to planting. Always rotate okra in the garden never planting in the same place more frequently than every three years.

A problem often encountered at blooming time is the losing of blooms without setting fruit. Okra, a member of the cotton family, blooms and pollinates the same day. The plant has perfect flowers. That is the male and female part of the plant is in the same flower. The pollen must fall or be carried to the female part of the flower. If this does not happen that day then the bloom is lost.

Sometimes the pollen is not released. It may be due to high humidity or unknown factors. When this happens the pod may try to develop. It will be a pod with nothing inside. Each seed in a pod must be pollinated, or it will not develop properly.

Sometimes when pollination does not occur, a fungus will attack the bloom. It will be moldy. It is not clearly understood whether the fungus attack is the result of non-pollination or whether this is a disease. A fungicide may be used.

There are many ideas as to the best remedy for the blossom not pollinating.

One of the old remedies is called "whipping" the plant. A stick is used to bruise and knock the leaves off the plant. This is not a scientific solution, but it may be that the whipping shakes the pollen loose and causes it to fall on the female part of the plant.

Another method is to pollinate by hand. A small soft brush is inserted into the bloom. It is very carefully used to loosen the pollen. It does not have to carry pollen from plant.

Another method recommended, and possibly the most logical, is to thin the leaves around the blooms. This will allow blooms to dry out quicker and to release the pollen.

Harvesting the fruit at the proper time is very important if the flavor is going to be at its best. The okra pods should be harvested about every other day. To determine if the pod is right for harvesting, break off the growing tip. If it is at its best, the tip will break off easily and clean. If it is too old, the tip will not break easily, and it will be ragged.

There is one insect that should be discussed. That is the stink bug. They attack the pods. They puncture the pod and eat on the inside. Most gardeners see the warts on the pod and think this is natural for okra. When these symptoms are seen it is too late. The damage has already been done. Stink bug damage can be prevented with a recommended insecticide.

OKRA Q & A

Q. The stalks of my okra look healthy, but the blooms fall off and no okra is produced. Sometimes a small pod will form, but it is completely hollow. What is the problem, and how can I control it?

A. The problem with your okra is that it is not pollinating. This happens even though the male and female portion of the plant is in the same bloom. The pollen, which is the male portion of the plant, must ripen and fall on the female part of the flower. When this happens, pollination takes place, and a fruit is formed. In your case, for some reason, the pollen is not being released. This may be caused by high humidity, or for some unknown reason. The small pods you found did not pollinate, thus no seeds were inside so development did not take place. Years ago, gardeners did what was called "whipping okra." They took a stick and literally beat the leaves off the plant and bruised the stalk. They probably knocked some of the pollen loose in the process. It is now recommended to remove the leaves around the blooms to allow better air circulation. Some gardeners take a small brush, insert it into the bloom, and turn it very carefully to break the pollen loose. It does not have to be carried from bloom to bloom. The parts in the bloom are very fragile.

Q. My okra has warts on the pods. Is this normal?

A. No. But so much okra has these warts many gardeners think it is normal. It is caused by an insect called the stinkbug. There are many variations of this insect. They damage the pod by injecting a toxic substance that breaks down the cell walls. They suck the juices back into their stomachs. The warts are the reactions of the plant to the substance injected. The problem is that many times the damage is done before the problem is recognized. This insect can be controlled with recommended insecticides. It helps to remove weeds near the plants, however the use of insecticides such as sevin is usually required.

Q. I have heard that okra is a plant that tells you when another application of nitrogen or complete analysis fertilizer is needed. Is this correct?

A. Yes, this is correct. Okra cannot talk, so it must give you the sign of what it needs. In this case, the sign is small blooms located in the top of the plant. Because okra produces over such a long period of time, it uses up the nutrients, especially nitrogen, and it needs to be replaced. This is done by side dressing about every 3 weeks with nitrogen or a complete analysis fertilizer high in nitrogen.

Q. My okra does well for a few weeks, but then it starts to turn yellow and dies. I don't see any sign on the plant. Can you tell me what the problem is?

A. Yes, I can. The problem is twofold. Most okra is resistant to a disease called Fusarium wilt. But, when the roots are attacked by nematodes, the resistance may be lost and the wilt kills the plant. The best way of reducing nematode numbers is to not plant this area for 3 years. All vegetation should be kept off. If it is an eroding area grass may be planted. There are some chemicals that may be used, but they are expensive. Research has shown that planting French marigolds will help. However, the entire area must be planted in the French marigolds, and no other plant be allowed to grow in that area. The number may be reduced by keeping the area plowed on whole growing season. This is especially successful if it is a hot dry summer. The nematode is killed if exposed to the sun for a few minutes. Nematodes will attack many other plants if they are planted in this area.

ONIONS

Onions may be produced from seed plants or sets. This is somewhat confusing to gardeners. Sets are small onions. Plants are small seedlings that are produced from seed and usually transplanted in the garden.

Onions produced for mature bulbs are usually planted in the garden in late winter. In warmer areas they may be planted as seed in the fall and carried through the winter. Onions are cool season plants, but they can be damaged or even killed by extreme cold.

Onions are set close together. They may be only 3 to 4 inches apart in the row and 12 inches between rows.

Onions are heavy users of fertilizer. They can produce many tons on an acre, so it is important to fertilize accordingly.

Making bulbs is a problem for some gardeners. One of the reasons for this is they treat onions like other plants. On most vegetable plants soil is thrown to the plant. In producing onions, soil should be pulled away from the plant continually until only one third of the onion is in the soil.

Onions are mature when the tops start dying in late spring or early summer. That is when they should be harvested. When a majority of the tops are brown, the remainder should be broken and all given an opportunity to turn brown.

Then onions should then be harvested and let dry in open air. If they are placed in the sun, cover lightly. The tops make a good cover. This prevents the sun from damaging the bulbs.

Once the drying process is over, cut or twist the top off about 2 inches above the bulb. Never remove flush with the bulb.

There are many ways of curing onions. One is to wrap individual bulbs in panty hose separating each one with a knot and hanging where the aeration is good. Another method is to spread them on hay where aeration is good. Mesh bags and slatted crates are usually used commercially.

Some onions store longer than others. The Vidalia or granex types don't keep like some other varieties. Special commercial refrigeration has been developed to keep these very popular onions lasting longer.

Gardeners frequently ask if they can produce Vidalia onions. They can be produced in areas where onions grow. Producers in the Vidalia area claim they have something in the soil that gives the sweet flavor.

There are insects and diseases that attack onions. They should be rotated as frequently as possible. Two of the major pests are onion maggots and thrips. The maggot is a soil insect that must be controlled in the soil. The thrip is a sucking insect that attacks the leaves. Both can be controlled with insecticides.

The diseases that affect onions include leaf spots, smudge and pink root fungus. These are fungal caused diseases that can be controlled with fungicides.

ONIONS Q & A

Q. I plant bulb type onions such as Texas Sweet and Vidalia. They do make bulbs like those I buy in the grocery store. Am I purchasing the wrong type of plants?

A. You are probably planting the correct varieties of onions, but are not following the correct cultural practices. The onions should be planted shallow. During the growing season the soil should be pulled away from the bulbs, until only about 1/3 of the bulb in in the ground.

Q. I have a problem with my onions forming a bloom on top. What can I do to prevent this as it seems to affect the taste?

A. This is called "buttoning" and is similar to "bolting" in the crucifers. It is thought to be caused by warm temperature during the seedling stage. It does not do any good to break out the tops. If they are at an edible stage you should harvest them.

Q. How do I know when my onions are ready to harvest?

A. Wait until most of the tops have died and fallen over. The remaining tops should be broken. They are ready to harvest when all the tops have turned brown.

Q. How is the best way to store my onions?

A. Some onions will naturally keep longer than others. The Granex varieties are difficult to keep over a long period of time. One method is to store them from touching each other. Remember, when harvesting to leave a short stem on the bulb. This helps prevent rot during storage. They may be spread out in an area of good circulation where they don't touch. They need to be kept in a dry cool place.

PEAS

When the term peas is used, in most instances, the reference is to cowpeas or, a term used in later years, Southern peas. Two other peas planted in the garden are the English pea and the sugar snap pea. The latter two peas are planted during the cool season, and the Southern pea is planted in late spring or early summer.

When the Southern pea market began to move out of the South a more appetizing name was given to them. Thus the name was changed from cowpea to Southern field peas. Many of the peas are still labeled cowpea, and, as a result, many people think they are mainly for cattle consumption rather than human consumption.

Southern field peas need a soil temperature of 70 degrees when they are planted. They are a legume and like a pH of 6 to 6.5, but they do not need much fertilizer. They are in the light feeder group. They need about one half the fertilizer used on medium feeders. They are probably the lightest feeders in the garden. Too much fertilizer encourages vine and not peas.

Peas are sometimes planted and mostly vines are produced. Many gardeners will tell you they were planted on the wrong time of the moon. Most horticulturists will tell you the soil is too rich. It seems that all of the nutrients do not have to be applied as fertilizer. Some soils are naturally rich, and peas can manufacture their own nitrogen because they are legumes. Some gardeners prevent this by planting peas in their poorest soils.

Southern peas should be planted about 4 inches apart and about one and one half inches deep. It is not usually necessary to inoculate Southern peas with nitrogen-fixing bacteria as they are already in the soil.

Southern peas planted too early will be badly damaged by thrips. This is noticed by the wrinkling and curling of the leaves. Slow growth rate seems to encourage thrip infestation. Peas should be treated for this insect.

Another major problem on peas is the cowpea curculio. This insect attacks immediately after the bloom falls when the pod is only a fraction of an inch long. For this reason, the peas should be treated with a recommended insecticide at five day intervals during the bloom stage. This usually requires about three applications.

If the curculio is not controlled the peas will be punctured for the insect to deposit its eggs. The term "stung" is used to describe peas that have been punctured. The small black spots may be noticed until the peas are being harvested or shelled. The peas in the pod will have a spot or may have a small worm.

Another insect that causes problems in peas is the aphid. Once this insect attacks complete stems will be covered. This makes harvesting quite uncomfortable as the aphid has a very soft body and is easily smashed. The aphid is not very difficult to control. Use an insecticide such as Malathion that has aphid on the label. Sevin is used quite frequently in the garden, but it does not control most species of aphids.

The main disease associated with peas is the pea virus. The best and only method of control is prevention. Plant varieties, such as Worthmore, that are resistant to virus. Also, it helps to keep fencerows free of weeds that harbor insects that carry the virus. These insects should also be controlled.

Selecting a variety to plant is difficult because there are crowders, creams and black. There are also dark peas, speckled peas, white peas and others. The best method is to plant a few varieties, and let the family decide which is the best tasting.

The best time to harvest peas is when the hull is bulging from the pea inside but before the hull begins to turn from its green to a yellow. They lose flavor quite rapidly.

Dried peas have been and still are a staple in the diet of many people especially in some of the poorer countries. They provide much needed protein for those unable to afford meat.

Pea weevils do a lot of damage to dry peas. One method of prevention is to heat the pea to 165 degrees

Fahrenheit before storing. This kills the eggs that may already be in the peas. They should then be stored in an airtight container to prevent re-infestation.

GARDEN PEAS Q & A

Q. Why do my neighbor's garden peas taste sweeter than mine?

A. Probably because your neighbor planted a different variety. The wrinkled varieties are sweeter than the smooth varieties.

Q. Do I need to stake my garden peas?

A. Not if you grow the determinate varieties. The indeterminate varieties grow taller and need staking. Also, the determinate varieties produce 2 peas from a bloom cluster, and the indeterminate varieties produce only one pea per cluster.

SOUTHERN PEAS Q & A

Q. Why do my peas go to vines and make very few peas?

A. Those who plant by the Almanac would say you planted at the wrong time of the moon. It may be that your soil is too rich or you over fertilized. Peas require about half the amount of fertilizer than other plants in the garden. In rich soil they may need no fertilizer at all.

Q. What is the difference between Southern field peas, and Cowpeas?
A. There is no difference. Pea farmers needed a more sophisticated name for Cowpeas, because many people thought they were only for cows. Today, some peas are simply called Cowpeas, but these are probably peas of unknown variety.

PEPPER

When the term pepper is used, it can mean a vegetable of many shapes, colors, sizes, sweetness or hotness. It all depends on the type of pepper it is. Some of the types are banana, bell, hot, sweet and pimento.

The banana pepper gets its name from the fact that it is shaped like a banana. Originally, banana was a sweet pepper, but now it is a sweet or a hot pepper. The color of both is pale green to yellow.

The bell pepper which is a sweet pepper is probably the most popular of all the peppers. Originally green, there are now red, yellow and chocolate varieties.

Hot pepper comes in all colors, sizes and shapes. Shapes range from banana shaped to a cherry shaped. Colors may match the rainbow with most being red, green or yellow. Some of these varieties are extremely hot, and, if touched, can cause burning to any part of the body touched with the hand. The hands should always be washed with soap and water after handling. Jokes should not be played with hot pepper, especially with the new super-hot varieties.

There are a number of insect and diseases that affect pepper. Two of these, cutworms and Southern blight, can be prevented as discussed in eggplants—that is, to wrap aluminum foil around the plant at planting time. The foil should extend two inches above and below ground level. Other insects include the European corn borer, blister beetles, white flies, horn worms and leaf miners. A control program using proper insecticides may be required to keep one or more of these insects under control.

There are also other diseases that cause problems with pepper. Some of these are bacteria wilt, fusarium wilt, alternaria, and virus diseases. To control plants with the wilt, rotate and pull out and destroy all infected plants. Chemicals will help prevent alternaria. To control virus, plant virus free plants and control weed and insects that carry the virus.

Pepper can have blossom rot just as watermelon and tomatoes. This is caused by a calcium deficiency. Spray with calcium chloride if the problem occurs. Lime should be applied if needed. Pepper should be harvested when it reaches the proper color and size. This is determined by the kind of pepper and the use to be made of it.

It is very important that pepper be rotated. It should not follow pepper, eggplants or tomatoes more frequently than every three years.

PEPPER Q & A

Q. My pepper has rotten spots on the bottom. Is disease the cause of this problem?

A. Not if it is leathery. It is caused by a calcium deficiency. It is called blossom-end rot. The pH should be 6 to 6.5. If the symptoms appear, spray with calcium chloride.

Q. My pepper dies suddenly. There are small white balls at the base of the plant. What is the problem?

A. As with other night shade family plants, this is Southern Blight. It can be prevented by wrapping the base of the plant with aluminum foil. For more information see the EGGPLANT section.

PUMPKINS

Pumpkins are vegetables that are used more for ornamentation and decoration than for food. This is true even though almost everyone knows about pumpkin pies.

Pumpkins are in the cucurbit family meaning that the male and female flowers are completely separate. Bees are a must for pollination. The male flower appears first causing many gardeners think they are not going to bear because the first blooms are all falling off. This is simply nature's way of making sure pollen is available when the female flowers are ready for pollination. This confusion can be averted if the gardener would become familiar with what the male and female flower look like. The small fruit appears on the female flower before the bloom. The male bloom sits directly on the stem.

Pumpkins come in many sizes. The miniature varieties may only weigh a few ounces, while the giant varieties may weigh over 2,000 pounds.

The seeds are a delicacy for some people. They roast them and eat them like roasted peanuts.

There are many different varieties of pumpkins. Each variety has a size, shape and color of its own. This distinguishes it from other varieties.

Pumpkins are produced on very prolific vines. The rows are usually wide because of this. The distance between rows is usually 8 to 10 feet, and the distance between plants is about the same. The seed are usually planted in mounds with about 5 to 6 seeds to the hole. They are thinned to 1 to 2 plants per mound.

Pumpkins are medium feeders. They like a pH of 6 to 6.5. It is best if the lime is applied the fall before planting in the spring.

PUMPKINS

Pumpkins are usually planted according to when the gardener wants them to mature. If Halloween and Thanksgiving is the goal, then they should be planted about the middle of June.

Weeds can be controlled by the conventional methods or chemicals. Once the vines begin to run, it is difficult to plow the row. Because of this a good weed control program should be started early. As the vines elongate, they will begin to pin down taking up water and nutrients. The runners may run 20 to 30 feet making it difficult for the main roots to provide these necessities.

In order to produce larger pumpkins, some gardeners leave only one pumpkin per runner. Some even thin to one pumpkin per vine.

Pumpkins like most of the cucurbits are attacked by many insects and diseases. Since pumpkins are kept for some time after harvest some diseases can do much damage after they are on the sales yard.

The insects that attack pumpkins include aphids, cucumber beetles, flea beetles, pickleworm, squash vine borer and squash bug. All of these insects can be controlled with chemicals, but some must be prevented. The pickleworm bores into the fruit, so an insecticide program must be used that prevents his entering. The squash vine borer enters the vine at ground level. It is difficult to control once it bores into the vine. The other insects may be controlled when observed on the plant.

The diseases that attack pumpkins include Alternaria Leafspot, Anthracnose, Gummy Stem Blight, Downy

Mildew and Powdery Mildew. All of these diseases can be controlled with a good spray program. However, the program must be started at the very first sign of the disease. Once the disease becomes well established, control is usually futile.

RADISH

Radish is the fastest maturing vegetable in the garden. It only takes 25 to 30 days for radish to be ready to eat. Many gardeners plant radish for this reason. Some think radish prevents insects from attacking other plants, so they interplant with radish.

They like a pH of 6 to 6.5. They are medium users of fertilizer. Radish may be planted in rows or in beds. They can be planted about one inch apart and about ¾ inches deep. It is best to make small plantings, so more plantings will make them available over a longer period of time. They tend to get hot as they get older. They are cool season plants, so they should be planted in the fall or early spring.

There are a number of varieties of radish. Most are round, but there is an icicle type that is elongated.

Insects and diseases are not usually a problem with radish.

Harvesting should be done when the roots are ¾ to an inch in diameter.

RADISH Q & A

Q. I have been told that radish is the fastest maturing plant in the garden. Is that the truth?

A. Yes, that is the truth. Radish will mature in about 28 days.

Q. Does radish interplanted in other crops repel insects?

A. Some gardeners say this is true, and they practice it in their garden. I have not seen any research to support this.

SPINACH

Spinach, the vegetable that Popeye made famous, is a cool season plant. It is planted in the fall or early spring. It is grown for its leaves which are very nutritious and tasty. It is planted alone or with other greens. It may be eaten cooked or in green salads. They are very healthy for the eyes.

Spinach prefers a pH of 6 to 6.5. It is a medium user of fertilizer. Most gardeners topdress spinach with nitrogen when it has been planted 3 to 4 weeks. Zinc and boron are minor elements needed by spinach.

It is the second fastest maturing vegetable in the garden, second only to radish. It matures in 40 to 45 days.

The preferred method of planting is in beds though some plant it in rows.

Weeds are not usually a problem since it is a cool season plant. They can usually be removed by pulling.

A good seedbed should be prepared. The seed, which are very small, should be planted 1 to 2 inches apart and ¾ inches deep.

The leaves should be harvested when they are large enough to make it practical. Most gardeners like to harvest when the leaves are 6 inches long. Spinach is attacked by a number of insects and diseases. The major diseases that affect spinach are anthracnose, cercospora and downy mildew. These diseases should be treated with a recommended fungicide at the first sign of the disease. The treatment should be repeated as recommended. Leaf miners and green peach aphids are the major insect problems. They can be controlled with insecticides.

SWEET POTATOES

Sweet potatoes are not the most popular plant in the home garden, but they can easily be produced in a garden setting. Some cultures depend on sweet potatoes for much of their food supply. They are a very healthy food being high in fiber.

SWEET POTATOES

The edible part of a sweet potato is not a tuber, but it is actually an enlarged root. This is why it is so important to harvest potatoes before the first frost. When the tops are killed by cold, the decomposing process moves on down into the roots and destroys them.

Sweet potato plants are started in hot beds. The seed potatoes are planted early enough so the plants will be ready to plant after the last killing frost.

Sweet potato plants should be planted on a broad bed. The plants should be spaced 12 to 15 inches apart in 3½ foot rows. Fertilizer should be applied prior to planting. They are heavy users of fertilizer. Some prefer to apply half of the fertilizer prior to planting and the other half about 6 weeks later.

Once the plants start to run, cuttings, called slips, can be removed and planted. They will need watering until roots have developed on the slips.

There are insects and diseases that attack sweet potatoes. Most of them attack the underground part of the plant.

Scab is one major disease that attacks the potato. It is not normally noticed until the potatoes are dug. Then rough spots are noticed on the potato. These spots penetrate the skin. They are difficult to sell even at reduced price.

Scab is best prevented. Plants should be produced only from disease free potatoes. All plants should be free of the disease when they are sold. Organic matter should not be added to the area where plants are to be planted.

Potatoes should not be planted where they have been planted in the last three years. Rotation is very important in the production of sweet potatoes.

Soil insects also attack the roots of potatoes. They must be controlled before the plants are put in the soil. This can be done using the proper insecticides.

The potatoes should be harvested when they are the desired size. They will keep producing until frost, however, as mentioned earlier, they will ruin quite rapidly once the tops are killed.

The potatoes should be plowed up once they have reached the desired size. Care should be taken not to bruise them during harvest. Those that have been wounded or bruised should be used as soon as possible.

After harvesting, they should be cured for 10 to 14 days at a temperature of 85 degrees. Once they are cured they should be placed in a cool dry place.

One method is to "bank" them—this is, to dig a hole 5 feet wide and 6 inches deep. Dig a trench farther out to drain away the water. Put down a layer of straw and a layer of potatoes. Make a cone out of plastic or tin. It will need to be supported. Continue the layers of straw and potatoes inside the cone. Leave the top open and cover with a removable weather proof cover. It helps the bank to breathe and provides a way to remove the potatoes as needed. The purpose is to keep them cool, yet keep them from freezing.

If you have only a few potatoes you may want to cook them and put them in the freezer. Also, a small volume may be placed in the coolest part of the basement on straw. They should be spread as much as possible.

SQUASH

Squash are divided into two categories. The two categories are Winter and Summer squash. Many gardeners, especially new ones, get these two terms confused. They associate the two terms with when the squash are grown. All squash are grown during the warm season. The difference is Summer squash must be processed while they are still immature. To keep, they must be frozen or canned. They can be kept for a few days in refrigeration. Summer squash varieties include Yellow Crookneck, Yellow Straightneck, Butterstick, Black, Golden, White Zucchini, Scallop, and others.

Winter squash will mature on the vine. They may be kept through the winter if they are allowed to mature, and kept from freezing. Baking is the preferred way of preparing mature Winter squash. However, when they are immature, they may be prepared in the same way as Summer squash—that is, stewed, casseroles, or fried. Varieties of Winter squash include Acorn, Butternut, Hubbard, and others.

Some gardeners refer to Winter squash as Vining type, and Summer squash as Bush. These characteristics better describe the reason for differences in planting systems.

The Winter or Vining squash seed are planted three feet apart, and the rows are spaced five feet apart. The planting depth is 1½ to 2 inches. It takes about ½ ounce of seed to plant 100 feet of row. That is planting 4 to 5 seeds per hill. After germination, they are thinned to 1 to 2 plants per hill.

The Summer or Bush squash are planted much closer together. They are spaced two feet apart, and rows are spaced 3 to 4 feet apart. The number of seed and the thinning is the same as for Winter squash.

Both Winter and Summer squash are medium users of fertilizer. They both like a pH of 6 to 6.5.

Traditionally, all squash have been planted in the garden as seed until the last few years. More and more seed are being started in the greenhouse and planted in the garden after the danger of frost is over. Plants may also be purchased in most garden centers. This gives the gardener the opportunity to have ripe squash earlier.

As squash season progresses, disease and insect problems increase. Vine borers, fruit worms, pickle worms, squash bugs, and others increase in number as the season progresses. When the problem becomes too severe, some gardeners dispose of the crop. Others turn to chemicals for control.

There are many insects that attack squash such as squash bug, stink bug, and others. The most damaging insect on squash is the squash vine borer. It is confused with disease because of the symptoms left by the insect. It attacks the plant at ground level. The plant begins to rot as a result of the insect entering the plant. Many times the damage is not noticed until the plant suddenly falls over. It appears as though the plant has simply rotted off. It takes close inspection to determine the damage was caused by a worm. The vine borer attacks the plant as soon as it gets a few inches tall. Applications of insecticides should start early. Pulling soil to the plant encourages the plant to put out new roots above the damaged area. This helps the plant to survive even after it has been attacked.

There are a number of diseases that attack squash. Some of these include leafspot, blossom blight, Downy mildew, powdery mildew, scab, and viruses. Most of these diseases can be controlled with fungicides except those caused by viruses. The viruses must be prevented through the use of disease free seed and the control of insects that carry the virus.

Weed control can be a problem with squash. They can be controlled with the usual methods such as mulching, hoeing, and chemicals, however there are few chemicals that can be used on the cucurbit family.

Being in the cucurbit family, the male and female blooms are separate. This causes confusion to some gardeners because they expect each bloom to produce a fruit. Less than 30% of the blooms may produce fruit since the male bloom cannot produce. It can only pollinate the female bloom. The male blooms appear first. The female bloom comes a few days later. Confusion will be minimal if gardeners will learn to distinguish male and female blooms. The female can be distinguished by their appearing on the stem before the bloom opens. The male bloom sits directly on the stem with no small fruit. Insects are required to take the pollen from the male bloom to the female bloom.

The male blooms are sometimes used for food. They are battered and fried. Some gardeners report them to be quite tasty.

Summer squash may be harvested as soon as they are large enough to make harvest worthwhile. They should be harvested daily. Winter squash may be harvested the same as Summer squash, or they may be left on the vine until the rind is hard. They can then be stored for the winter in a place where they will not freeze.

Squash will produce over a long period of time if the mature fruit is removed from the plant. If they are not removed the plant will cease to produce new blooms and fruit.

SUMMER SQUASH Q & A

Q. My squash start bearing prolifically and then break off at ground level. Sometimes I touch one walking by, and the whole plant breaks off at the ground. What is the problem?

A. Many people are confused by this problem. It appears to be a disease has rotted the plant off. Actually, this was caused by an insect. The squash vine borer bored into the stalk at the ground weakening the plant. The plant breaks at that point. The prevention of this insect is not easy. A number of insecticides are recommended such as Sevin and others. They are applied to the base of the plant every 3 to 5 days. Some have even recommended injecting the base of the plant with a hypodermic needle. They use one of the above insecticides. Some gardeners pull soil to the plant each time they work in the garden. This encourages root growth above where the plant may have been attacked. It is also important to plant as early as feasible in your area.

Q. My squash bloom profusely, but it is a long time before they start to hold the blooms. What can I do to prevent this?

A. Not very much. Squash are in the cucurbit family. The male blooms which are separate come on the plant first. Nature has provided that they have pollen ready before the female bloom comes on. For more information on this, refer back to CANTELOUPES.

WINTER SQUASH Q & A

Q. Can winter squash really be grown in the winter?

A. No, they get their name from the fact that they have a hard rind and can be stored through the winter if they are kept from freezing. They are also called vine squash since they run like cucumbers and watermelons.

Q. How do I know when winter squash are ripe?
A. They can be eaten any time after they come on the vine. The young squash are usually fried or used in casserole. The squash is mature when the rind is hard to the fingernail. Most varieties also change colors.

SUNFLOWERS

Many gardeners plant sunflowers in the garden. There are many different varieties and sizes of sunflowers. The one most often used in the garden is the giant variety. This sunflower may have a seed head 12 inches or more in diameter. There are small varieties used for oil and bird feed that have much smaller heads.

Sunflowers should be planted after the soil has warmed up. May is a good month, however they can be planted much later. They should be planted in 30 to 36 inch rows and 8 to 10 inches in the drill. They are medium users of fertilizer. Split applications of fertilizer should be used or topdress with nitrogen when they are 18 inches tall.

Weeds may be controlled with any of the methods recommended for the vegetables. Due to their height, thick canopy and competitiveness, weeds are not usually a problem except when they are small.

SUNFLOWERS

There are a few insects and diseases that affect sunflowers. Mildew is usually the worst problem. This can be controlled with fungicides.

The insects include sunflower moth, corn earworm and stink bugs. All of these can be controlled with insecticides.

The seed head of a sunflower is heavy when mature. They tend to hang down. Care should be taken to prevent them from falling over. The seed heads may be left on the plant until they turn grey and will readily shell out. At this stage they can be protected from insects and birds by covering with a mesh material. When they are dry they should be stored in a dry place inside until they are used.

TOMATOES

Tomatoes are probably the most popular plant in the garden. Many gardeners are satisfied with tomatoes being the only plant in their garden.

They are planted for a number of reasons. First, they are to be used for food. They can be used in so many different recipes. A few examples include sliced tomatoes, cut up in salads, stewed, fried green, many sauces, canned, frozen, pickled, and many more.

All of this for a vegetable that no one would dare touch many years ago. The reason is tomatoes were thought to be poison.

Many gardeners plant tomatoes to see how big a fruit they can produce. In many cases, the quality of the fruit is not important, only the size.

Some are grown to set a record on the number of tomatoes that can be produced on one plant.

The major division of tomatoes is based on growth habit. They are called determinate or indeterminate.

Determinate type tomatoes have a much shorter growing season than the indeterminate type. Not that it produces faster, but its production period is much shorter. It produces about six weeks, and then it dies. This reduces the need for staking because the plant never gets very tall.

Indeterminate type tomatoes have a longer growing season. It will grow as long as conditions are favorable for growth. Some grow as long as 20 feet. They produce well into the fall if they are properly managed. Sometimes they are grown until frost, and the green tomatoes are picked, and placed in a cool area. As they are needed, they are put in a sunny window where they ripen. The gardener is rewarded by having fresh tomatoes well into the winter.

Tomatoes are usually planted in the garden as plants. Seed are usually planted in the greenhouse 6 to 7 weeks before the last killing frost. This gives them time to get big enough to plant in the field after the last frost. This puts the gardener six weeks ahead in production time. Some gardeners plant in the field well before the last frost. They have developed ways to protect the tender plants from the cold. Some of the more primitive methods include covering the plants on cold nights with milk jugs, hay, straw, newspapers or other suitable material.

Some of the more sophisticated methods of protection from cold include miniature plastic tunnels or greenhouses over the rows or surrounding the plant with a plastic material. This material is filled with water which absorbs heat in the day time and keeps the plant from freezing at night.

Tomatoes are heavy users of fertilizer. The row should be fertilized and limed prior to planting. For best results the lime should be applied the prior fall. The fertilizer can be placed to the side of and below the plant. In this case, to avoid burning the roots, half the fertilizer should be applied at planting and the other half six weeks later. Another method is to broadcast all the fertilizer at once. Tomatoes should be side dressed every three weeks during the growing season. They produce so abundantly over such a long period of time, the nutrients, especially nitrogen are constantly being used up by the plant.

When tomatoes are planted in the field, they are usually tender and subject to being broken by the wind. Some plant producers harden their plants off before placing them on the market. However, many do not. Because of this, it is wise to plant the plant half in the soil. Fewer plants will be broken by the wind, and a better root system will be established.

Indeterminate types should have their supports put down at planting. This prevents disturbing the root system at a later date. The support mechanisms vary almost as much as growers of tomatoes.

Some prefer to use a simple stake driven into the ground at the base of the plant. They prune off the suckers and tie the plant to the stake as it grows.

Another method of support is a two foot circle made out of concrete reinforcement or some other type of wire. This is placed over the plant. The suckers should also be removed if this method is used.

Some prefer to use a square made out of 1 x 4's. This type of structure should be about 2 feet wide and 5 feet high. The boards should be spaced 6 to 10 inches apart.

Another method is to lay wire horizontally over the plant about 18 to 24 inches above the ground. A second wire should be placed the same distance above the first wire. Hog cattle or dog wire may be used. The plant may need a little help getting through the wire initially, but once through the problem is solved.

Most garden centers sell baskets made out of wire that can be pushed down over the plant while small. It is more difficult if the plant is over about 2 feet tall. These baskets may be purchased in different sizes.

The prior mention of suckers may be somewhat confusing to those who have not had experience growing tomatoes. The sucker is the shoot that comes out at the axel of the leaf. That is between the leaf and the stalk. Be sure when removing these they are not confused with the blooms. The sucker is easily rooted in sand or water. They will produce quicker than young plants. Some gardeners use these to start a fall crop of tomatoes.

As the plants grow, they should be observed for insect and disease problems. Treatment should be started at first sign of either. Side dressing with nitrogen should be started as soon as the first tomatoes are about the size of a dime. Apply about 2 tablespoons per plant every three weeks as long as they are producing.

Some of the insects that affect tomatoes include cutworms, fruit worms, tomato hornworms, stinkbugs, aphids, mites and others. Insecticides may be used to control these insects. The cutworm can be prevented by placing aluminum foil around the plant at planting time.

There are also many diseases that affect tomatoes. The first precaution is to purchase plants that are resistant to as many of these diseases as possible. Many plants are labelled VFN resistant which means they are resistant to verticillum wilt, fusarium wilt and nematodes. There are many other diseases such as bacterial wilt, Southern blight, early blight and others.

Early blight can be lessened by mulching and keeping soil from splashing the leaves. There are also a number of fungicides that can be used to prevent or lessen the severity. Southern blight can be prevented in the same manner as recommended for cut worms. The fungus that causes this blight is an oxygen loving fungus. It must attack the plant at ground level. The aluminum foil placed on the plant for cutworms forms a barrier that keeps the fungus from getting to the plant above the ground. Southern blight can be diagnosed by a wilting of the plant and small pustules at the base of the plant.

Bacterial wilt cannot be controlled once in the plant. The first symptom is a complete wilting of the plant in 24 to 48 hours. To determine if a wilted plant has this wilt, cut a four inch section from the plant and extend it 2 inches into a glass of water. If it has this wilt a cloudy stream of sap will be seen in the water.

There are also fruit rots that affect tomatoes. These rots are best prevented by applying a mulch about 4 inches deep to keep the fruit from contacting the soil. These include fusarium, rhizoctonia, and pithuim. Southern blight may also attack the fruit.

There are two diseases caused by a virus that attack tomatoes. These are tobacco and cucumber mosaic. Both of these are carried by insects which should be controlled for prevention. The tobacco mosaic is caused by people handling the plants after handling tobacco. A person who smokes or chews tobacco should wash their hands in milk before handling tomato plants. All infected plants should be pulled out and destroyed.

There are other problems that affect tomatoes that are confused with diseases. One of these is blossom end rot. That is a darkening of the underside of the tomato. The skin will have a leathery feel. This problem is caused from an insufficient supply of calcium. In some cases, the calcium is in the soil because the area has been limed, but it is not available to the plant.

The calcium may not be available to the plant for a number of reasons. Some of these include damaged roots, drought, excessive moisture, nematodes, heat and many others.

Treatment for this condition, once observed, is to spray every 12 to 14 days with calcium chloride. This provides needed calcium through the leaves, and it may be taken through the roots. It helps to mulch the plant. This keeps down soil temperature and helps keep soil moisture level. Liming prior to planting, preferably 3 to 6 months, helps prevent the problem. Some suggest the addition of gypsum at planting helps.

Catface is sometimes confused with disease problems. Catface is inherent in some plants but may also be caused by improper pollination. Each seed in a fruit must be pollinated or the fruit will be malformed.

A problem gardeners see in early spring is the dropping of blooms. The cause is usually cool weather. Anytime the temperature drops below 55 degrees Fahrenheit, blooms will not set. The same happens in mid-summer when the temperature goes above 95 degrees.

Harvest tomatoes when they have turned red, pink or yellow, depending on which variety they are. The flesh will be soft but still firm to the touch. The yellow varieties are not as acidic as the red ones.

TOMATOES Q & A
Q: What does the term "determinate" or "indeterminate" mean when used to describe tomatoes?

A: It describes the type of vine that variety will produce. The determinate variety does not have to be staked. It usually grows to 5 to 6 feet and stops. The indeterminate type keeps on growing to as much as 16 to 20 feet. Because of this, it needs to be staked.

Q: My tomatoes turn black on the bottom end. It seems tough and does not rot like most diseases. What is wrong?
A: It is not a disease. It is a calcium deficiency. The plant is not taking up enough calcium. It may be because there is insufficient calcium in the soil, or some other factor is preventing the plant from taking up the calcium. It may be caused by insufficient moisture or heat. Once the problem is noticed spraying with calcium chloride at 12 day intervals will correct the problem. Prevention includes making sure the pH is correct, mulching to lower soil temperature and to keep soil moisture constant.

Q: Last year my tomatoes split. I would like to prevent this from happening this year. What can I do?
A: Tomatoes split because of excessive moisture, usually following insufficient moisture. High rates of fertilizer may also cause this. Try to keep moisture constant and don't over-fertilize.

Q: What causes the center of my tomatoes to be hard and white?
A: This may be hereditary, or it can be from over-fertilization.

TURNIPS

Turnips are planted for the greens and the roots. They are probably the number one greens in the South. They are very easily and quickly produced. Greens can be produced in 45 days and can be planted in the fall or spring. They can be planted in the spring when the worst freezes are over. They can take some cold weather. In the fall, they should be planted after the hottest weather is over and early enough to make before the first freeze. Some gardeners say that a little frost enhances the flavor.

A good seed bed should be prepared. They can be planted in rows or broadcast. The seed are very small. There are plants that can be used in garden planters to plant rows. To broadcast, they can be mixed with sand, lime or meal. There are also spreaders especially designed for small seeds.

Before planting, lime should be applied to bring the pH up to 6 to 6.5. The lime will work quicker if worked into the soil. Lime moves downward very slowly. Also work the fertilizer into the soil. Fertilizer with a ratio of 10-10-10 or 5-10-15 may be used. Topdressing after three weeks will provide needed nitrogen and keep the plants growing. The faster the growth, the more tender the greens.

Insects and diseases can be a problem, especially for those planted in the fall. It is best to wait until cool weather to plant.

The main insects that attack turnips are aphids and cabbage loopers. Aphids can be a problem even after a number of frosts. Both of these insects can be controlled with insecticides. The looper is harder to kill. The biological control agent Bacillus thuringiensis will control this insect.

The major diseases are those that cause spotting of the leaves. These include anthracnose, cercospora, downy mildew and pale leafspot. Like most diseases, it is easier to prevent them than to control them once they are established. Fortunately, fungicides will prevent all of them.

A spray program should be started when the plants are 2 to 3 inches tall and continued until harvest.

The leaves may be harvested when they are 5 to 6 inches long. The larger the plants, the more greens that will be produced. If they are thick, the plants may be thinned as used to allow more room for the roots to grow. If they are broken off, they will continue to produce more leaves. The roots may be harvested when they are 1 to 1½ inches in diameter.

Some gardeners throw soil to the roots when the weather gets cold. This protects the roots from freezing. They may keep well into the winter.

TURNIPS Q & A

Q. When is the best time to plant turnips to produce roots?
A. Fall planted turnips make the best roots. It is also important to plant a variety that produces roots.

Q. I have had healthy turnips that developed spots on the leaves and finally died. Is this a deficiency, or what causes this?
A. It is caused by a fungus. It may be Cercospora, Fusarium or Powdery Mildew. These diseases must be prevented. Once the infection is heavy, there is not much chance of cure. At the first sign of the disease, spray with a fungicide.

WATERMELON

Most gardeners like watermelons, but, under normal production methods, they take up a lot of space. Some innovative gardeners construct a trellis for the plant to run on. They prepare a special structure on the trellis to hold the melon. The melon can also be suspended in a mesh bag.

Watermelons are in the cucurbit family. They have male and female blooms separately on the same plant. The fruit, which is in front of the bloom of the female flower, is visible before the bloom opens. Because the blooms are separate, bees are a must for pollination purposes. Some commercial producers rent beehives to put in their fields during the pollination process.

Watermelons should not be planted until after the danger of frost is over. Plants planted prior to the last frost grown in the greenhouse are becoming more popular. When the greenhouse plants are used, melons will be ripe a few weeks earlier. Prices are usually higher on the early market.

Seeds or plants should be planted on a broad bed. They should be planted in 10 foot rows and 6 to 10 feet in the drill. The plants should be planted the same depth they were planted in the nursery, and the seed should be planted 1½ inches deep.

There are many different colors (rind and meat), sizes and even seedless melons. Some rinds are gray, light gray, light green, dark green, striped and solid. The meat may be red, yellow or golden. The size may range from 5 to 150 pounds, depending on the variety. Bigger fruit may be produced by thinning to one melon per runner.

Watermelons are medium users of fertilizer. One popular method of applying fertilizer is to put down half at planting time and the remainder in two or more applications. They also respond to pop up fertilizer. Other elements that may be needed are boron, sulfur and zinc. A pH of 6 to 6.5 is desirable.

Once they are planted, they should be kept free of weeds. Since the rows are so wide, it is easy to plow the middle. There are also herbicides that can be used.

Rotation is very important to prevent diseases. However, a good spray program will prevent diseases if started early enough. Prevention is the key word. Gummy stem blight, downy mildew, powdery mildew, anthracnose and nematodes can wipe out a field of watermelons.

Watermelons are also subject to blossom end rot. This is caused by a calcium deficiency. They will respond to calcium chloride, but, because of their fruiting habits, they will not respond as quickly as tomatoes. Apply lime 3 to 6 months prior to planting. If gypsum is available, apply at planting to help provide calcium.

There are a number of ways to determine if a watermelon is ripe. One way is to check the tendril nearest the fruit. If it is dead, then the plant is ripe. Another way is to look underneath the melon to see if it has turned yellow. If it is, then the melon is ripe. The favorite for old time producers is to thump the melon. If there is a dull thud, the melon is ripe. If the sound is a sharp thud, then the melon is green. Practice at this leads to perfection.

WATERMELON Q & A

Q. What causes my watermelons to turn black on the blossom-end?

A. Same as for tomatoes above. It is blossom-end rot. It is caused by a calcium deficiency. You should spray with calcium chloride at 12 day intervals. For more explanation, see tomatoes.

Q. Why do my watermelons have so many blooms, but so few melons?

A.   Watermelons like cantaloupes, cucumbers and pumpkins, have male and female flowers. All the male flowers can be eliminated where a fruit is expected. Only the female flowers will produce a melon, and they must be pollinated by the pollen from the male. Remember also that a vine can only support so many melons. Beyond this point the melons will be reduced in size. For larger melons, remove some of the blooms or fruit.

Carl Brack, Sr.

The author of this book is Carl Brack, Sr. He was born in Portal, Georgia and graduated from Portal High School in 1953. He attended ABAC College at Tifton, Georgia. He then attended the University of Georgia where he received a Bachelor of Science degree in Forestry in 1960. He later went back to the University of Georgia where he received a Master of Agriculture Extension in 1969. Mr. Brack served his country by joining the National Guard in 1953. He served in the Guard for nine years. His primary job during his eighty years was with the University of Georgia Cooperative Extension Service where he served for almost thirty years.

Made in the USA
Monee, IL
31 March 2021